'What are you weaving?'
'Time'

Authors: Lesley Millar, Takeo Uchiyama, Chiyoko Tanaka
Series Editor: Matthew Koumis
Project Manager: Keiko Kawashima
Translator: Kaeko Nakagawa
Graphic Designer: You. Kobayashi
Reprographics by Fotoriproduzioni Grafiche, Verona, Italy
Printed in Italy by Grafiche AZ

Published by
Telos Art Publishing
PO Box 125, Winchester
SO23 7UJ
England
telephone: +44(0)1962 864546
facsimile: +44(0)1962 864727
e-mail: editorial@telos.net
U R L : www.arttextiles.com

© Telos Art Publishing 2002

ISBN 1-902015-24-X (softback)
ISBN 1-902015-42-8 (hardback)

A CIP catalogue record for this book is available from
The British Library.

Photo Credits:
Yoshiaki Shimooka, pages 5, 18, 20, 30
Morio Kanai, pages 26, 28
Akira Koike, pages 21-25, 32-41
You. Kobayashi, page 45

Artist's Acknowledgements:
This book is dedicated to my parents.
Special thanks to Teruko Sugiyama, Atsuko Masazumi
and James Rehm

Publisher's Acknowledgements:
I would like to thank Jorie Johnson who first introduced
me to Chiyoko Tanaka in Kyoto, 1997. Thanks also to
Keiko Kawashima, You. Kobayashi and Simone Crivelli for
their boundless patience during the production of this
book. MK.

Front Cover Illustration:
Permeated Black – Black Stain On Deep Green Stripes #53 (1990)
hand-woven fabric (ramie, silk, cotton), rubbed with
charcoal, black-dyed
photo by Akira Koike

Back Cover:
Grinded Fabric – Red Stripes, R #10 (1988)
hand-woven fabric (ramie), rubbed with brick
photo by Akira Koike

Portfolio Collection volume 12

Chiyoko TANAKA

Foreword

Prior to the 1973 Lausanne International Tapestry Biennale, contemporary Japanese textile art had been marginalised. But the six Japanese textile artists who exhibited at that exhibition revealed radically new styles, liberated from the restrictive framework of traditional textiles. Hitherto, traditional tapestry had been two-dimensional and confined to the wall. But the new work broke from this tradition, being three-dimensional, incorporating a wide variety of materials such as wood and metal, and employing a wide variety of techniques such as knitting and binding.

The international reputation of Japanese textile art blossomed, the medium gaining in vitality and popularity in Japan during the seventies. In contrast with a conceptual approach to fine art, textile artists at that time relished the sheer hands-on physicality of making. But some fundamental questions still needed to be addressed about the nature of weaving and of dyeing.

Several artists were exploring these questions, among them Chiyoko Tanaka. Her starting point had always been a very individual one; she was not allied to the general stance of 1970s textile art which, broadly speaking, explored sculptural aspects in textiles. Since the 1980s the public has been able to see the fruits of Tanaka's inquiries which may be summarised simply: she articulates her woven cloth as an accumulation of time. The warp is covered by the weft, and the warp gradually disappears over time during the weaving process. I would like to explore this further with two examples.

It was Tanaka's 1984 series, entitled *Grinded Fabric*, which sealed her reputation. Here, she traces the texture of the earth through a process which she refers to as *grinding*: this involves spreading a woven fabric on the ground and then rubbing the surface with a stone or brick. The act of *grinding* also symbolises the passage of time, the artist even

attempting to capture the future through rubbing the fabric, as the texture of the earth is transferred onto the cloth, or, in other words, as the fabric is marked by a subtle but profound imprint of the earth. As a result of *grinding*, some areas were left literally threadbare, thus exposing the warp which had been concealed by the weft. Tanaka's work unveils the essence of reality, too often concealed by wordly illusions.

The *Permeated Black* series appeared in the late 1980s. In it, she dyed threads which had been wound onto a cylinder so that the outer layers of thread became darker than the inner layers. She subsequently wove this unevenly-dyed thread as weft, the resulting woven cloth having subtle gradations of black. This is one of the processes Tanaka uses to symbolise the passage of time. She combined two elements of passing time, dyeing and weaving, to form an expressive fabric.

I would like to conclude with some general observations. Tanaka's work is informed by the environment of Kyoto, ancient capital of Japan, where she lives and works. I often see a glimpse of ancient buildings such as a tea-ceremony room, in her works. I would say that Tanaka's intimacy with nature gives her an awareness of the tempo of nature, which forms the basis of her work.

Takeo Uchiyama
Director
The National Museum of Modern Art, Kyoto

日本のテキスタイル・アートが世界から注目を受けるように
なったのは、1973年、スイス、ローザンヌの国際タピストリー・
ビエンナーレで6名の日本人作家が入選して、それまで全く知
られていなかった現代の日本のテキスタイル・アートが新鮮な
魅力をもって迎えられたことによる。当時のローザンヌ国際タ
ピストリー・ビエンナーレではタピストリーの、平面で壁に掛
けられるという従来の概念を破り、レリーフ状や立体作品が登
場し、また機で織ることなく、編んだり、括ったりという織り
以外の技法により、素材でも木や金属など糸以外のものを用い
る作品も見られた。つまりアートとの壁を破った新たなテキス
タイル・アートが登場したのである。

　欧米で日本のテキスタイル・アートが認知されたことによっ
て、70年代には日本でもこの分野が急に活気づいた。アートの
世界ではコンセプチュアル・アートが盛行していたから、テキ
スタイル作家が喜々として手を動かし、自由に作品を造ってい
く様は実に新鮮に映ったものである。

　しかし70年代末にはテキスタイル・アートの世界にもコンセ
プチュアル・アートの思考が影を投じてくる。織りとは何か、
染めとは何かを問う作品が生まれてきた。既成の布を何枚も重
ねて切断し、それによって生じる断面や糸のほつれをそのまま
提示することで布の本質を示す作品や、染めた布をほぐして、
糸の染まった部分と染まっていない部分を示すことで染めとは
何かを示すというような作品が生み出されていた。

　1980年代から作品を公に発表し始めた田中千世子も70年代の
テキスタイルによるフォルムを求める行き方とは異なり、織る
ことは何かとの問いを出発点としている。綴織技法によって作
品を作っていた彼女は、その答えを織りとは緯糸が経糸とから
み合い乍ら、次第に経糸を見えなくして行く時間の堆積である
と解いた。80年代から90年代にかけて彼女の活動は活発だっ
たが、基本的にこの織りとは時間の堆積であるという思考を基本
としているのである。

　田中千世子の作品を強烈に印象づけたのは1984年の 'Grinded
Fabric' のシリーズであろう。織り上げた布を地面の上にひろ
げ、上からレンガや石でこすることによって地面の表情を写し
とるのである。彼女にとっての布は過ぎ去った時間の堆積であ
り、それを再びこするという行為、これも時間の堆積であるが、
また布が今後過していくであろう時間を先取りして示すのであ
る。写しとられた地面は微妙で奥深い表情を布に与え、所々擦
り切れた箇所からは緯糸によって隠されていた経糸が覗いてい
る。過去が再び呼び覚まされ、しかも未来をも暗示しているの
である。また田中千世子は個展でギャラリーの端から端まで二

left:

1 | Grinded Fabric – Ocher #300-1
| 1984

right:

2 | Grinded Fabric – Ocher #300-2
| 1984

枚の長い布を並列的に並べたこともあった。一枚は織られた布
をこすり、さらに黄土をのせたもの、もう一枚は実は織られた
布ではなく、ギャラリーの壁から壁に床上に糸を張り黄土を撒
いて糸を隠したもの。つまり彼女の織りに対する基本的考えを
直截に表したものと言えよう。

　田中千世子は80年代の終わりから黒染め織りを発表するよう
になったが、そうした織りのなかには筒状の巻かれた糸を染料
につけ、染めむらのある糸を用いた、黒のグラデーションのあ
る布がある。これも染まると言うことが染料が浸みて行く時間
の現れであり、そうした過去の時間を再び織るという時間の堆
積のなかに融かし込んでいるのである。

　田中はこうした今日的な造形思考を作品に示しているがそれ
は彼女が育ち生活する、日本の古都京都と無縁ではないように
思う。その作品は時に古建築や侘びた茶室を思わせ、制作の根
底には、人が自然と密接に結びつき、しかも全ては移ろい行く
ものという思考があるように思うのである。

京都国立近代美術館　館長
内山　武夫

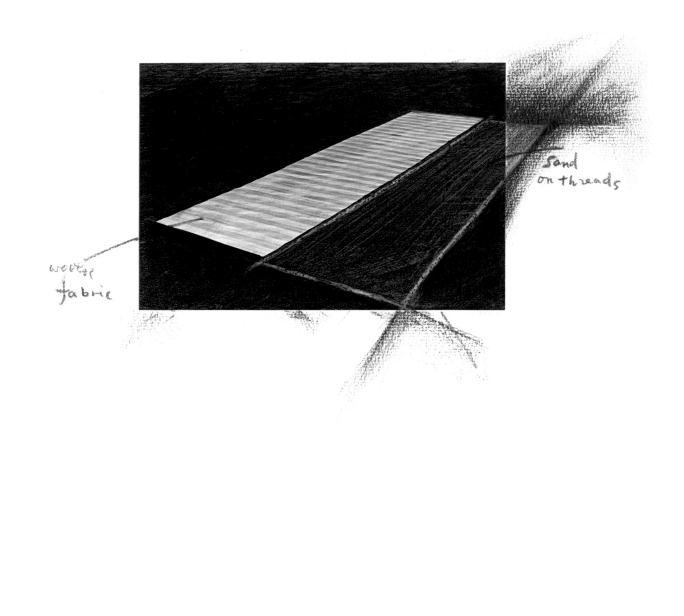

woven
fabric

sand
on threads

Contents

At the Still Point: Time Present and Time Past[i]   *Lesley Millar*

To fully appreciate the integrity of Chiyoko Tanaka's woven and stitched textiles we should try to understand the importance of Time within her work. Artists have always been drawn to the concept of time. For the most part they have been less concerned with recording time, but more interested in the intensity of their personal responses to the ideas surrounding it, seeing things as if for the first time, exploring aspects of time in different ways. Time can be experienced as linear, hierarchical, textural, ephemeral and mortal. For Tanaka her woven fabrics are the locus of time, both describing time and taking time. Her work is linear – the warp and the weft; it is hierarchical in terms of process; it is textural through the materials; its ephemeral and mortal nature is exposed through the 'grinding' process. Time can make manifest the scale of experience and her stitched *kesa* works represent and contain aspects of memory and mortality.

The surface qualities of the work reflect Tanaka's spiritual and physical relationship with her surroundings. Chiyoko Tanaka lives and works in the mountain forest on the northern edge of Kyoto, the 1,200 year old, former capital of Japan where the Nishiki woven silks originated. The silks, distributed through the Silk Road, and collected and stored among the Shosoin Treasures[ii], are still being woven today, providing visible evidence of a continuum of practice. The loom on which Tanaka weaves is not so very different from those that have been used since ancient times, and through her work she assumes a conscious connectedness with this practical and spiritual heritage, producing material evidence of the threads of time.

Chiyoko Tanaka's preoccupation with time extends throughout all aspects of her work. We can see this in her precisely timed drawings of Stonehenge, which, by the nature of the drawing, indicate the passage of light (time) through her methods of determining the fall of the shadow. There are close affinities within the drawings between the shapes drawn; they are not seen as separate pieces of stone, more as pointing to their primordial status, emerging from the same genus. The interlinking relationship of the stones within this ancient monument, whose very purpose (it is claimed) was to announce certain moments in time, has been identified by Tanaka through her drawing. As some in the West turn to the East to discover a meditative wholeness, Tanaka shows us that, within our landscape, there is a tradition 'built from a rich deposit of myths, memories and obsessions. The cults which we are told to seek in other native cultures – of the primitive forest, of the river of life, of the sacred mountain – are in fact alive and well and all about us if only we know where to look for them.'[iii]

In this essay I will be looking at two of the approaches taken by Tanaka in her work and the relationship they have with each other. As she says 'I feel my woven work and the *Kesa Series* are two ways of dealing with the same thing – time and the human condition.' Tanaka is most known for her woven permeated and grinded fabrics as illustrated in, for example, *Six Squares Indigo Blue* and the *Permeated Black* series. Her fabrics have their starting point in the dying of the yarn. I have noted in a previous essay[iv] that the cone of yarn is dyed in its entirety, allowing the dye slowly to permeate the thread, the resulting graduation of colour becoming a visual indicator of time. In her use of black, she creates luminosity by underpinning the black with another colour. The deep understanding of black, demonstrated by Tanaka, is rooted within traditional Japanese aesthetics and practice[v]. In Tanaka's work we can see a range of symbolism reflecting the use of cloth within a complex society 'from its ancient beginnings to its myriad uses in rituals of continuity and despite the competition of fashion and factory, its contested retention as an anchoring point, a link to real and imagined

　田中千世子の織られたり、綴られた布による作品にふれ、その世界を鑑賞するには、そこに「時間」という要素が深くかかわっていることを理解する必要があるだろう。つねに芸術家たちは時間という概念に強く惹かれてきた。ほとんどの場合、彼らは記録としての時間よりも時間に対する個人的な関係に興味を持ち、さまざまなやり方で時間の様相を探索し、表現してきた。そして、時間を、連続し、積み重なり、形成し、移ろい、消滅するものとして経験することができるといえよう。彼女にとっての織られた物とは、この流れゆく時間の軌跡そのものなのである。経糸と緯糸の連なりが、だんだんと織られ、積み重なり、物質としてのかたちを有し、さらに「擦る」行為を通して移ろい変わってゆく様があらわにされる。一方、時間を記憶の重なりとしてとらえることもできよう。綴られた布による袈裟シリーズの中では、過ぎ去った時への追憶と同時に、運命の未来をもひとつに包含して示している。

　これらの作品は、彼女が育ち制作している京都、北山杉が茂る洛北の地と深くかかわりあっている。千二百年の歴史を持つ古都、京都では、シルクロードを経て伝播した正倉院御物[ii]に見られる錦などの絹織物が、営々と織られており、今まで受け継がれてきた伝統の絹織物を目のあたりにすることができる。彼女が使っている機も昔のそれとさほど変わらず、長く培われてきた伝統とその精神性を意識する環境の中で制作をつづけている。

　田中千世子の時間に対する強い関心は作品が制作されてゆく中で、さまざまに展開される。このことは、描かれた時刻が一枚毎に記されていった一連のストーンヘンジのドローイングにも見られる。彼女にとってこのドローイングとは、そこに落とされた影を描いてゆくことであって、それは同時に、光の移行——時間の経過を描いてゆくことになる。時刻の記されたドローイングから、そこに描かれている形が単に石の塊として見られているのではなく、これらの石の太古に立っていた状況をも同じように示して描かれていることがわかってくる。先史時代の遺跡のストーンヘンジの石の並べられた意図は、ある特定の瞬間を指し示すための位置に配置されているというが、移行する光と影を描き、時刻を示してゆくこのドローイングの行為にも同じ意図が認められるといえよう。

3:20 pm, 29th April, 2001, Stonehenge

3:35 pm, 29th April, 2001, Stonehenge

5:50 pm, 29th April, 2001, Stonehenge

roots of the past.'[vi]

'Fabric' rather than 'cloth' is how Tanaka describes her work, and 'fabric' shares its linguistic root with 'fabricate': to construct or make. The process of weaving, the construction of the fabric, is central to her work. She speaks about 'the beautifully stretched warp being covered by weft threads, one after the other – the simple reality of the relationship between warp and weft threads as a construct.' In the development of the work she sets up a vertical time axis – the warp – and a horizontal space axis – the weft. For her, the weaving process is one of transformation. The crossing points of warp and weft physically disappear from view as the work progresses but continue to exist as integral to the fabric. An accumulation of weft threads, one by one, representing time passing, the finished cloth existing in time present.

After weaving the fabric, it is laid out on the ground and Tanaka begins the process she calls 'grinding'. To do this she uses, for example, red brick from Sienna, as illustrated in *Three Squares. Blue Threads and Sienna. #281*. The brick is rubbed into the back of the fabric until it permeates the material, changing its colour. At the same time the face of the fabric takes on the patina of the ground, thus she is able to trace out the texture of the ground while grinding out the surface. Through the grinding she is saturating the material with the cumulative response of the stone and the ground beneath, which have combined with the threads to become the fabric itself, reflecting the energies of the 'grinder'. The entire process is reinforced by the structural integrity imposed by the constraints of the warp and weft. In 'Landscape and Memory' Simon Schama writes of 'an excavation, beginning with the familiar, digging down through layers of memories and represenations toward the primary bedrock, laid down centuries or even millennia ago,

and then working up again toward the light of contemporary recognition.'[vii] When Chiyoko Tanake rubs the sand into her cloth, through her actions she becomes part of the continuum which began with the pebbles rubbing together until they became the sand that she is using to re-establish that primal contact with the earth. Her approach is one of ritual, during which there is a transference of spiritual significance between her as maker and fabric as object/outcome.

At times her approach can be seen as relating directly to performance. Her *Grinded Fabric – Ocher #300* is an installation of two weavings, one of which has been produced by hand rubbing the upper surface with white stone and applying Jurakadai soil [viii], exposing the blue ramie warp threads and embedding the ochre soil in the fabric. The second fabric in this installation is created by laying an unwoven warp of blue ramie on the floor and fixing it at both ends. Then, in an enacting of the process of weaving, Tanaka spreads the soil over the warp until it is eventually covered. Initially this work was also made with Jurakadai soil but in subsequent installations she has used soil or sand from the region where the work was being exhibited. Thus the piece has been 'made' anew for each exhibition, creating a different time/space existence to its material partner within the installation, demonstrating Tanaka's ability to take textiles into the realm of performance art. When Andy Goldsworthy creates his clay works which cover the wall or floor these works 'should feel as if they have risen to a building's surface as a memory of its origin, a connection between the building and its material source.'[ix] Tanaka's work, particularly *Grinded Fabric – Ocher #300* constructs a similar evocation of elemental forces through the embedding, drying and cracking of the soil together with her continuous re-creation of the piece.

西洋のある人たちが東洋に精神の調和を見いだしたように、彼女は私たちの風景の中に、「神話や、記憶や、妄想の幾重にも積み重なった層からたちあがって伝承されてきたものがあり、その土地特有の原生の森、生きている川、神聖な山に対する畏敬の念は、私たちが、それらに出会える場所を知っていれば、いつでも、ごく身近なところで感じることができる。」[iii]と、私たちに教えてくれている。

　この評論では田中千世子の作品の制作に対するアプローチについてと、各シリーズとの間にみられる相互の関係に焦点を合わせてみようと思う。彼女がいうように「私にとって、織りによる作品とか、裂裟シリーズの作品とか、各々表現の方法は異なりますが、私が見ようとしていることはひとつで、時間とのかかわりをもつさまざまなもののあり様そのものなのです。」本書にも掲載されている 'Six Squares, Indigo Blue' の Grinded Fabric（擦られた織物）シリーズや、Permeated Black（浸みてゆく黒）シリーズが特によく知られているが、Permeated Black シリーズのプロセスは、糸の染まってゆく時点から始まる。筒状に巻かれた糸を、そのまま黒の染液に浸けて、黒の染料がだんだんと巻かれた糸の表面から内側へと浸透してゆく。この染まってゆく時間の経過として、黒のグラデーションがあらわれてくる。私が前の評論で述べたように、[iv]彼女は、グラデーションに染まった緯糸の黒を各々わだたせるために、赤と青の経糸を使いわけて織っているが、赤下黒や青下黒といった他の色を併用して黒を用いるこのような黒に対する深い知識は、日本の長い伝統に培われた美意識に根ざしているものなのである。[v]「古代、布が使われ始めた頃より受け継がれている日常の習慣の中での多くの布の使われ方は、現代のファッション産業が盛んであるにもかかわらず、布の役割を堅持して、昔からある実際的かつ象徴的な布の役割は今日まで続いている。」[vi]と述べられているように、次第に複雑になっていった社会の中で、布がどのように扱われてきたかを暗示し表わす象徴主義との関連が、これらの作品の中にもうかがえる。

　田中千世子は織られた作品を 'cloth' というよりも 'fabric' であると説明している。というのは、名詞の 'fabric' の言語学的ルーツは 'fabricate' という「作る又は構成する」の意味を含む動詞に由来するからなのである。彼女のいう「美しく張られた経糸が緯糸によってだんだん見えなくなってゆく、この経糸と緯糸のあり様。」つまり、織りのプロセス、織りの構造が作品の制作の中心に位置づけられていて、垂直方向の経糸を「時間」ととらえ、水平方向の緯糸を「空間」ととらえている。時間としての経糸は織ることによって視界から消えてゆき、それと同時に一本一本の緯糸が積み重ねられて、過ぎゆく時間の軌跡としての織物が、目の前にあらわれてくる。

　この織り上げた織物を地面に拡げて表面を「擦る」。たとえば 'Three Squares, Blue Threads and Sienna #281' では、レンガを使って織物の表面を擦る行為を通して、レンガによって表面が擦り取られると同時にレンガの色がくい込み、地面のテクスチュアーを織物のおもての面に写し取るのである。また、石を使って擦る行為を通して、石に伝わってくる織物の下にある地面の手応えを感じ、地面に接している織物のうらの面に、地面のテクスチュアーを押して凹凸をつける。こうした一連の擦るプロセスが、経糸と緯糸からなる織物本来の構造をあらわにしてゆく。サイモン・スカーマによる「風景と記憶」には「発掘という作業は、何世紀、何千年もの過去に遡り、幾重もの層の記憶を掘り下げるという作業によって、この記憶を現在の認識の範疇の地点にまで呼び戻すという行為である。」[vii]と述べられているように、彼女が、織った物に土などを擦る行為からは大地と原始の根源的な接触をよみがえらせて、この行為と一体となり、つくり手の彼女とつくられた織物との間には精神の交感が見受けられるように思う。

　さらに田中千世子の制作行為がパフォーマンスとして見られる 'Grinded Fabric － Ocher #300' は二つの織物による床の上のインスタレーションである。二つの織物のうちひとつは、織物の表面が、聚楽第の土[viii]と一緒に石で擦られ、土が表面にすり込まれていて、経糸の青い先端を見せている。もう一方は、床の上に青い経糸が壁から壁へと張られて、あたかも織るかのように、緯糸としての聚楽第の土が青い経糸の上に端から撒かれ覆われている。最初のインスタレーションを構成していた二つの作品は、同じ聚楽第の土が使われていたが、その後に展開されたインスタレーションでは、撒かれた土による作品は、展示された場所の周辺から土や砂を探して用いた。

In her stitched works, which she has titled *Kesa Series*, Chiyoko Tanaka is moving into areas more overtly concerned with identity. Within many societies there is a 'centrality of cloth to gift exchange at marriage and death, the beliefs in its affective, spiritual powers – its capacity to bless and protect – and its evocation of continuities, however fragile, with the past.'[x] The *Kesa Series* were begun at a time of loss, the deaths of her father and mother, which precipitated what she calls 'an emptiness in my mind'. Into this emptiness she began to layer memories of her parents and through this began an equivalent layering of the cloth. As these works were created soon after her parents' death, each of the *Kesa* illustrated contains The Lotus Petal which, within Buddhist thought, represents Heaven and Peace.

A traditional kesa is a garment worn by a Buddhist priest, it is a rectilinear fabric made up of many pieces of cloth stitched together in a particular format. Buddhist priests are allowed no possessions, and, according to tradition, the most appropriate cloth would have been made from soiled or discarded rags. In practice the scraps would originally have been the clothing of others, sometimes very beautiful silk kimonos, and would have been donated for the purpose. Central to this was the transference of identity through the cloth. In Tanaka's *Kesa Series*, the identity of the original owners of the cloths used is unknown to her. It is the fact that the cloth has been worn, used, and therefore contains the trace elements of the wearer, the owner, which imbues the scraps of fabric with meaning. The cloth itself is worthless, it is the accretion of memory which, for Tanaka, gives the cloth its value.

Traditionally, the making of a kesa was an act of devotion in itself, the stitched quilting needing careful concentration, while prayers (or mantras) were quietly repeated at each stage[xi]. The stitching within Tanaka's *Kesa Series* carries further meaning. The overall dynamic of each work is one of centring, descending and vanishing, and the stitching pattern is used to emphasize the downward and centring energy of each piece. To balance this downward movement, there are elements at the sides and top of the work. A 'vanishing point' is also represented by the crossing line at the centre of *Three Squares. Blue Threads and Sienna. #281*.

The original Sanskrit name for kesa, kasaya/kashaya, actually means 'turbulence' and refers to the process of dyeing fabric. It might even be that the act of dyeing a fabric in itself was sufficient for making it suitable for a kesa.[xii] Also, the term kashaya, when applied to colour, refers to mixed, neutral or earth tones, with connotations of impurity and uncleanliness[xiii]. Tanaka describes this 'dark or dirty colour as a visualisation of the determination to be free from worldly desire.' I have already discussed the importance of dyeing as a manifestation of time within her work, and although the amount of dyeing she applies to these *Kesa* works is more of a dark stain made from Chinese ink (Sumi-zome) or mud (doro-zome), it is there to emphasise and balance the downward energy of the stitching.

Octavio Paz writes that craftsmanship provides a continuity between past and present, the artisan allowing himself to be vanquished through time; throughout her work Tanaka is seeking not to conquer time, but to be at one with its flow[xiv]. The grinding process is one in which she reveals the essential nature of the fabric, and as we see the erosion, so we understand the continuity contained within the material, the process, the place and time. There are however, points in that continuity, achieved through her use of the ground itself as 'a plate from which I extract an engraving', which describe a certain moment in time, a particular place, a unique surface. The overall surfaces she creates can be seen to be descriptions of a process that has passed, but

各地のインスタレーションにおいてその場所の土や砂との関係を提示して、設置されるたびに新しく「時間と空間」との関係を創り出すことによって、田中千世子はテキスタイルをパフォーマンスアートの域にまで持ち込んだといえよう。アンディー・ゴルズワージーは壁や床を粘土で覆った作品を発表したとき、「覆われた表面から、その建物と覆った粘土の素材そのものに付随している本来の記憶が、あたかも浮び上ってきたように感じてほしい。」と述べた。[ix] 彼女のくり返し設置してきた‘Grinded Fabric － Ocher #300’は土が埋め込まれて乾きそしてひび割れた表面によって、アンディー・ゴルズワージーの作品と共通の感情を観るものに呼び起こす。

田中千世子が袈裟シリーズとよんでいる綴られた布による作品は、彼女の関心がアイデンティティーという領域に著しく移行しているのがうかがえる。日本では、さまざまな社会の慣習の中に、「昔から受け継がれてきた布の役割が残されている。たとえば結婚のお祝いの品を納めるときとか、葬儀のとき供物を供えるときの布の役割などは、葬式や信仰のきまりごととして、大切に守られ残されている。」[x] この袈裟シリーズは、彼女が両親の死に接し、心にできた虚空に両親のおりおりの想いを重ね、思い出としての着物や、仏教の浄土を象徴する蓮華の花びら文様の古裂などを使い最初の作品が生まれてきた。

袈裟とは儀式に僧侶たちが身にまとう装束であり、制定された形式に従って、いく「条」かの帯状の布を綴り合わせた長方形の布であるが、元来は衣服に対する欲望を制するために、用のなくなった古い布の断片を継ぎ合わせて修行僧の衣としたのが原形であった。それらの布の断片は、以前には誰かの衣服であったし、時には着物を打敷に仕立て替えて、寺院に奉納することがあった。つまりここに布を通してアイデンティティーの移行がみられる。袈裟シリーズに使われている布には持主はっきりしないものもある。しかし、大切なことは、それがかつて使われていたことで、すでに用のなくなった布ではあるが、時を経て、さまざまな痕跡が残されている布として、再び彼女にとって意味をもってくる。

もともと袈裟のために布の小片を綴り合わせてゆく作業は、一心に経を唱え、静かに一針ずつ刺しすすめられたのである。[xi]

一方、彼女の袈裟シリーズの作品に見られる縫い目による線には、独自の強い意味づけがされている。各作品の画面は、その中心へ向う動きと、下降し消えてゆく動きが意図され、この縫い目による斜線が、中心点へと集中する方向と、下降する方向を強調して指し示している。この下降する力を表わす黒の逆三角形に対応して均衡を保つかのように、上部と左右両端に小片の布が配されている。一方、中心への方向を示す二本の斜線の交叉した交点は、「消点」として意図されたもので、同じこの「消点」は、‘Three Squares, Blue Threads and Sienna #281’の作品の画面の中心に、斜の一本の青い糸とこれに交わる鉛筆で描かれた斜線によっても表わされている。

袈裟とはサンスクリット語の‘kasaya/kashaya’にあたり混濁した色を意味し、[xii] 衣服への執着を断つために濁った赤褐色に染めるのが原則であった。その色から僧侶の衣を袈裟と称するようになった。[xiii] 私はすでに彼女の作品が制作されてゆく中での時間とのかかわりを表わすものとして、染めの重要性について述べたが、袈裟シリーズの中で見られる墨染めや泥染めは、墨や泥水を下へ向かって垂らしにじませることによって、縫い目の斜線によって示された下降する力をさらに強調してもいる。

オクタビオ・パズは、熟練した技能とは過去と現在の時を継ぐ役割を果たし、そしてまた職人はこの時間によって自分自身の感情が抑制されてしまうと書いたが、彼女の制作姿勢からは、時間を克服しようとするようなところは感じられず、むしろ時の流れと共にあるのがわかる。[xiv] 彼女の擦る行為は織物としての本質的なあり様を目で見られるようにし、私たちはこの表面を目のあたりにすることによって、素材とのかかわりとか、制作する行為とその場所と時間との密接な関係を理解するのである。ある場所の地面を、あたかも版画を刷るための版のようにして、その地面に織物を置き擦る行程をおこなう。この経過した時間のしるしとして現れた表面は、素材としての意味を越え、あらたな意味をもって存在する。現れた微妙な表面のテクスチュアーは、地面から写し取った地表の微視的な模様を見せ、絶え間なく移りゆく光によってより一層きわだって見える。これらの作品にふれるときには、そこに残された過去の時の跡に私たちの現在の時を重ねて流

they also carry the implication that they can be inscribed with meaning outside the material itself. The extreme subtlety of texture created becomes apparent through minute shifts of light, revealing a microscopic picture of the earth's surface. As with all her work, the importance of allowing ourselves time to look, in a manner of a contemplative progression across this revealed surface, cannot be too highly stressed. Chiyoko Tanaka's work, in its movement from one state to another, can heighten our awareness of the course of time, which moves alongside us, neither looking for death, nor denying it, but accepting its place in the cycle of renewal.

Tanaka's work is essentially regenerative, she is taking her materials – linen, sand, used clothing – on a further journey and allowing us to take part in this spiritually and visually rewarding transformation. There are links with felt and paper making, in that the fibres and inherent structural relationships are altered, almost alchemically, to create an entirely new fabric through the process of change. Paz again points out that 'the aesthetics of change requires that each work of art be new and different from those preceding it; novelty in turn implies the negation of immediate tradition.'[xv] For Chiyoko Tanaka there is an acknowledged continuity between past and present; her work emerges from, and contains, what has gone before. At the same time, her creative and genuinely innovative, interventionist approach places her work at the forefront of contemporary practice.

Lesley Millar
Daiwa/AHRB Research Fellow
The Surrey Institute of Art and Design, University College

i. T.S. Eliot, *Four Quartets: Burnt Norton* (Faber and Faber, 1944)
'At the still point of the turning world. Neither flesh nor fleshless;
Neither from nor towards; at the still point, there the dance is,
But neither arrest nor movement. And do not call it fixity,
Where past and future are gathered.'

ii. Within the Todaiji temple complex in the city of Nara, there is the 8th century, wooden, Shosoin building. Shosoin served as the repository for around 9,000 temple treasures dating as far back as the 7th and 8th centuries including many from overseas, reflecting the silk road from China to the Mediterranean. For this reason Shosoin is called the Treasure House of The world.

iii. Simon Schama, *Landscape and Memory* (Fontana Press, 1996) p14.

iv. *Textural Space* Catalogue: 'Curators Introduction' (The Surrey Institute of Art and Design, 2001) pp5,6.

v. 'There is a black which is old and a black which is fresh. Lustrous *(brilliant)* black and matt black, black in sunlight and black in shadow. For the old black one must use an admixture of blue, for the matt black an admixture of white; for the lustrous black gum *(colle)* must be added. Black in sunlight must have grey reflections.' *Hokusai, John Cage, Colour and Meaning* (Thames & Hudson 1999)

vi. Jane Schnieder and Annette B. Weiner, *Cloth and Human Experience, Introduction*, with reference to final essay in collection by Louise Cort: 'The Changing fortunes of Three Archaic Japanese Textiles' (Smithsonian Institution Press, 1989) p20.

vii. Schama, op.cit. pp16,17.

viii. Jurakadai soil comes from an area of the same name, in the Kyoto region. It is used as a wall surface within traditional Japanese houses and tea houses.

ix. Andy Goldsworthy, *Time* (Thames & Hudson, 2000) p8.

x. Jane Schnieder and Annette B. Weiner, *Cloth and Human Experience. Introduction*, with reference to final essay in collection by Louise Cort: 'The Changing fortunes of Three Archaic Japanese Textiles' (Smithsonian Institution Press, 1989) p19.

xi. Barry Till and Paula Swart, 'Elegance and Spirituality of Japanese Kesa', *Arts of Asia* Vol.27, No.4, p55.

xii. *op.cit* p54.

xiii. Alan Kennedy. *Japanese Costume: History and Tradition: Kesa, The Essential Buddhist Garment* (Éditions Adam Biro, 1990) p123.

xiv. Octavio Paz, *Convergences. Seeing and Using: Art and Craftsmanship* (Bloomsbury, 1987) p61.

xv. *op.cit* p60.

れにたゆたってみたい。ひとつの段階から、また別の段階への行程は、私たちにそっていつも流れてゆく時を思い出させ、時間についての認識を新たにさせてくれるのである。それは、死をみつめるでもなく、死を否定するでもない、ただ生命の根源から死に及ぶ生命の全円環をめぐる点として時間を受け止めることになろう。

　このように田中千世子の仕事の根底には再生流転の認識があり、麻や砂や古い布などの素材をはるかな旅へといざない、同時に私たちを精神的、視覚的に応え報いる変化への道づれにする。フェルトや紙づくりのプロセスにも共通しているが、繊維であることと繊維に本来備わっている構造上の関係が変えられて、まったく違った新しい織物が創り出される。いわば繊維の錬金術といっていい。こうした転化のプロセスを経て、あらたな織物が新しい意味の光をあびて姿をあらわしてくる。オクタビオ・パズは「変化の美学とは、各々の作品が新しく、先行するものとは異なっていることを要求する。その斬新さとは、目前の伝統の否定を暗に意味する。」[xv]と指摘している。そして一方、田中千世子は、現在と過去の時、過去と未来の時が、集合されている廻転する世界の静止点において、ひとつのかたちを残す。深い思索と、つねに自らの世界を発展させてきた創造性が、その作品を、今日、ひとつの本質的な存在として位置づけているといえよう。

大和振興財団研究員、サリー芸術大学
レズリー・ミラー

i. T.S・エリオット（著）「四つの四重奏曲」バーント・ノートン、西脇 順三郎（訳）
「廻転する世界の静止点において。肉体でもなく肉体でなくもない、
　　どこからでもなく、どこへ向って行くのでもない、
　　　その静止点には舞踏がある。
　しかし止められもせず運動もしない。でも
　　それは固定されているとはいえない、
　　　そこでは過去と未来が集合されている。」

ii. 正倉院は、奈良にある東大寺内に位置する、8世紀に建てられた木造建築。正倉院は、7世紀、8世紀にさかのぼる約9,000件の正倉院宝物の倉庫であり、中国から地中海にいたるシルクロードから来た宝物が収められている。正倉院が世界の宝庫と呼ばれているゆえんである。

iii. サイモン・スカーマ（著）「風景と記憶」（フォンタナプレス、1996）p.14

iv.「素材空間」展覧会カタログ：キュレーターによる序章（サリー芸術大学発行、2001）p.5, 6

v.「くすんだ黒と鮮やかな黒があります。輝く黒と光沢がない黒、日光に照らされた黒と影の中の黒。くすんだ黒には青を、光沢がない黒には白を使わなければならない。輝く黒には膠を加えなければならない。日光に照らされた黒にはグレイの反射光が必要です。」
北斎、ジョン・ケージ（著）「色とその意味」（テムズアンドハドソン発行、1999）

vi. ジェーン・スキニーダー、アネットB．ワイナー（著）「布と人間の経験」序章、ルイズ・コートコレクションによるエッセイ：三つの古代日本の染織の変化の運命（スミソニアン博物館発行、1989）p.20

vii. サイモン・スカーマ（著）「風景と記憶」p.16, 17

viii. 聚楽第土というのは京都にある同じ名を持つ地域に由来する。この素材は伝統的な日本の家屋や茶室の壁土に使われる。

ix. アンディー・ゴルズワージー（著）「時間」（テムズアンドハドソン発行、2000）p.8

x. ジェーン・スキニーダー、アネットB．ワイナー（著）「布と人間の経験」序章、p.19

xi. バーリー・ティル、ポーラ・スワルト（著）「アートアジアVol.27, No.4」日本の製裟の品格と精神、p.55

xii. 同書、p.54

xiii. アラン・ケネディ（著）「日本の衣装：歴史と伝統：裂裟、仏教徒の基本的装束」（アダム・バイロ編集、1990）p.123

xiv. オクタビオ・パズ（著）「収束、見ることと使うこと：芸術と工芸」（ブルームズベリー、1987）p.61

xv. 同書、p.60

Chiyoko TANAKA

Mud Dyed Cloth Series

I see my work as 'being in' or 'visualizing' a world I have perceived, or I am trying to perceive. This is the reason that I am trying, through my working process, to transform the inherent logic of time into the inherent logic of space and vice versa. I consider that the use of Mud becomes the transformation of material being into time — Mud dyeing is a permeating process, enabling a transformation of time coherence into space.

wall:

3 | Grinded Fabric –
Six Squares, BG, Charcoal #402
1985

floor:

4 | Permeated Black #400
1986

5 | Bengara #501
| 1984

6 | Missing Mud Cross #764
| 1991

Printed & Grinded Fabric Series

The corrosive action of printing on a plate can be understood to represent the transformation of material unity into time. Through the creation of the surface, which has spatial dimensions, the act of printing becomes the transformation of time into space.

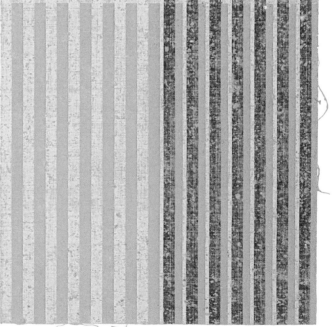

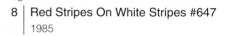

left:

7 | Red Stripes On White Stripes #646
page 25, top left: detail
1985

right:

8 | Red Stripes On White Stripes #647
1985

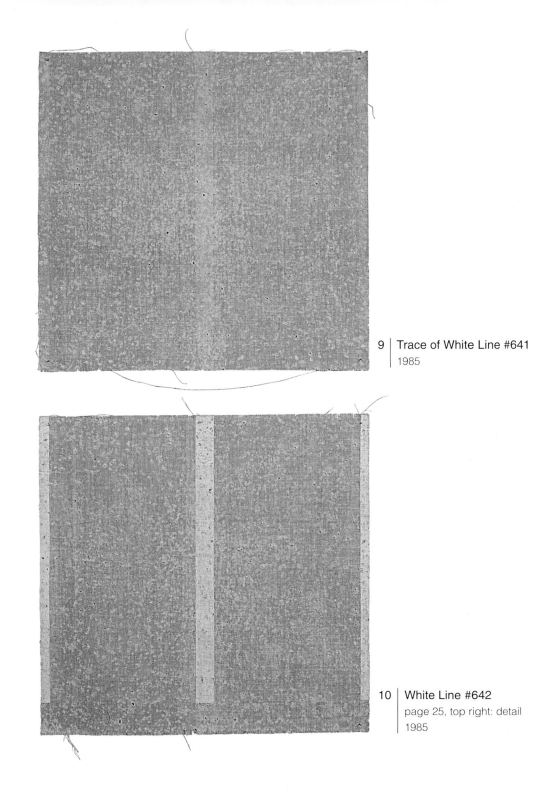

9 | Trace of White Line #641
| 1985

10 | White Line #642
| page 25, top right: detail
| 1985

11 | Trace of A Leaf #151
opposite: detail
1988

Grinded Fabric Series

above, upper:

12 | Six Squares, Indigo Blue, W #306
1994

above, lower:

13 | Six Squares, Indigo Blue, RF #305
1994

For me the act of weaving, as the weft threads accumulate one by one, is a representation of time passing away; texture acting as the locus of the present time. Finally a piece of fabric is the result, the existence of which I regard as the expression of my sensitivity. To be specific, weaving for me should be the process of transforming the weft into accumulated space, replacing the vanishing time. Placing the fabric on the ground, I trace out the ground texture and grind out the surface of the fabric. The act of tracing is a transformation of time coherence into space and grinding is the transformation of space coherence into time. The final colour of the surface is not so important, more the effect achieved by the application of a certain soil, charcoal, or choice of tool which helped translate the texture of the ground more readily into my 'canvas'. The true past tense of the verb to grind, ground, also implied the earth, which can be used to embed, implant, erode and emboss its own surface into my work.

12 | Six Squares, Indigo Blue, W #306
detail
1994

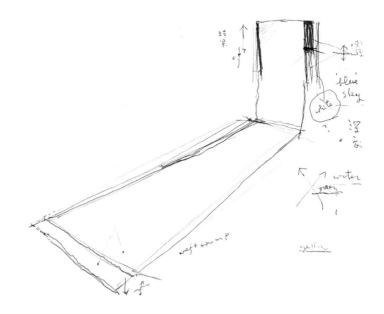

When I began to weave, a friend asked me,
'What are you weaving?'
and I remember answering,
'I am weaving time.'

wall:

14 | Blue #100-2
1983

floor:

15 | White, B #100-1
1983

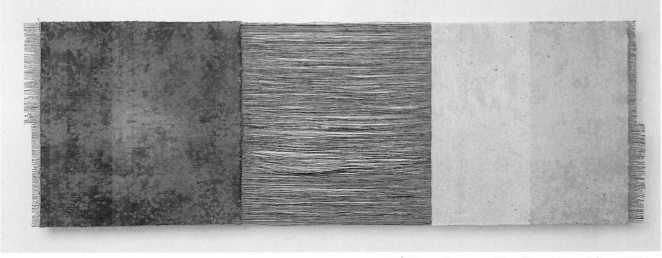

17 | Three Squares, Blue Threads and Gray #671
| 1997

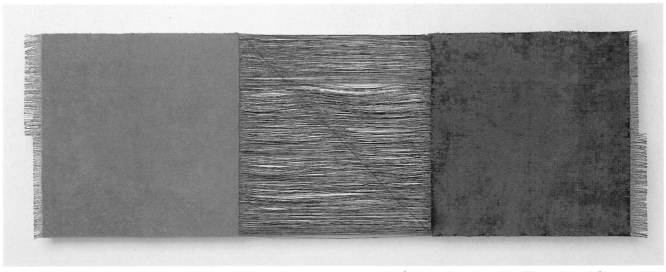

18 | Three Squares, Blue Threads and Sienna #281
| 1997

left:
16 | Red Stripes, R #10
| 1988

Permeated Black Series

19 | Black Stain On Deep Green Stripes #53
| 1990

20 | Black Stains On Deep Green Stripes #52
| 1990

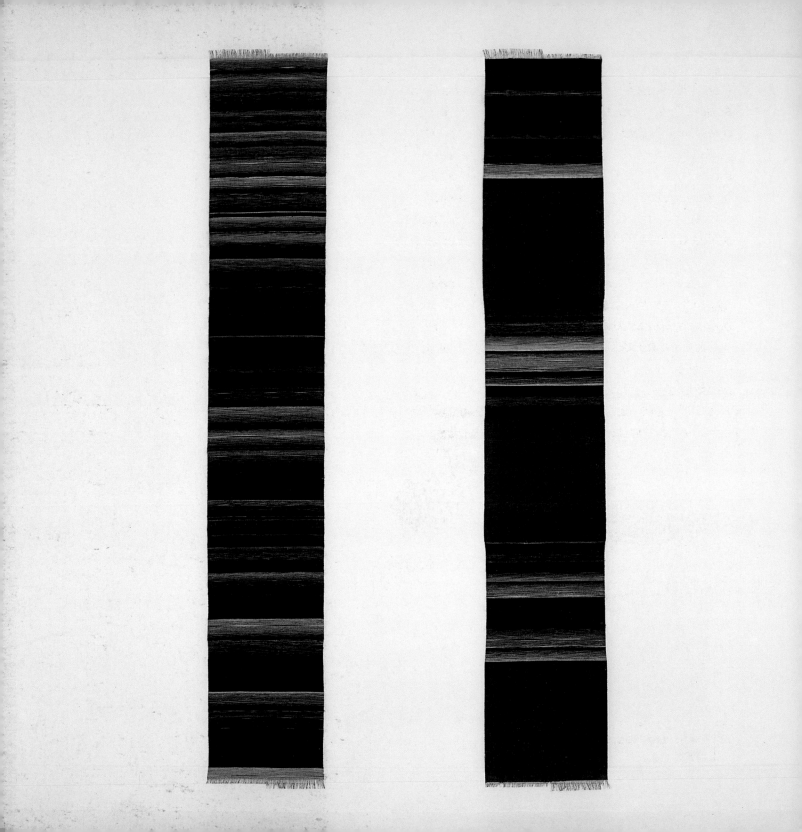

I see dyeing as a transformation of time into space, the permeating process of black dyestuffs, resulting in a graduated black. This series consists of two processes. The woven piece, symbolising the passage of time, is laid outdoors on the ground. When black dyestuff is poured on the centre of the piece the dye moves outwards, permeating the woven piece and leaving black stains as the trace of passing time. For the second piece, I wound threads onto a cylinder and dyed them, so that the outer layers became darker than the inner. I then used these threads as weft, creating a woven piece whose gradation of black has become the trace of passing time. Though the use of these threads and the permeated black dyestuff, both these works combine two indicators of time passing, dyeing and weaving.

right, detail of weaving, previous page, far left:

21 | Black Gradation #903
     | 1990

previous page, weaving on right:

22 | Six Squares, Black Gradation #904
     | 1990

Kesa Series

Man is mortal, one's individual identity vanishes instantly at the moment of death. I was with my parents for their ending time and I found that I had a large emptiness in my mind. I laid an occasional memory of my parents on it, hoping a new horizon in my life would materialise. From this effort, the Kesa series started and continues. I collected fragments of old, worn cloth and sewed them together adding some design elements, for example, dyeing with Chinese ink (sumi-zome) or mud and stitching. For me, used cloth holds memories and this expresses my basic concept of time being changed into space and space into time.

23 | *Sange*, Lotus Petals #97-1
1997

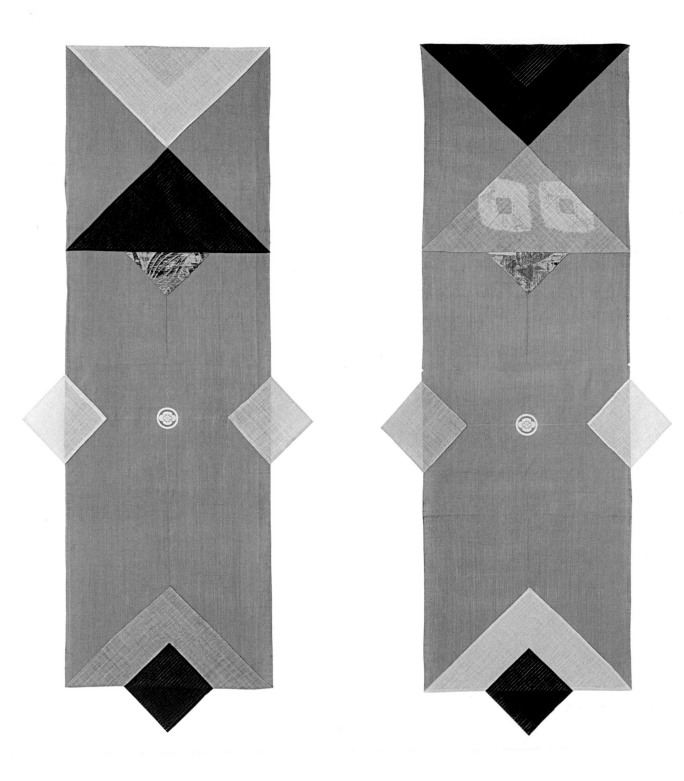

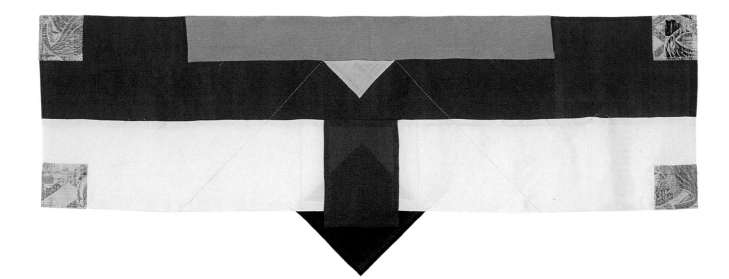

26 | *Sange*, Lotus Petals #98-1
   | 1998

Biography

Born   1941, Tokyo, Japan

Education and Awards

1959-63 BFA, Kyoto City University of Arts

1963-65 Postgraduate Textiles, Kyoto City University of Arts

1988   6th International Tapestry Triennale, Lodz, Bronze Medal

Selected Solo Exhibitions

1981   Gallery Gallery, Kyoto (also in 1984, 85, 86, 87, 88, 89, 90, 91, 92, 93, 95, 98, 2002)

1982   Gallery Miharudo, Tokyo

1986   Ryo Gallery, Kyoto

1987   Gallery Maronie, Kyoto

2002   Art Life Mitsuhashi, Kyoto

Selected Group Exhibitions

1987   *Expression/Construction of Filament*, Spiral, Wacoal Art Center, Tokyo

          The Exhibition of Selected Artist '87, Kyoto Municipal Museum of Art, Kyoto

1988   *Art Now '88*, The Hyogo Prefectural Museum of Modern Art, Kobe

          6th International Tapestry Triennale Lodz '88, Central Museum of Textiles, Lodz, Poland

1992, 93 *Kohyama and Tanaka Contemporary Ceramics and Textile Art from Japan*,

          Museum het Princessehof, Leeuwarden, The Netherlands (tour Germany, Japan)

1993   *Applied Art collected by Benno Premsela*, Stedelijk Museum, Amsterdam

1993, 94 *Focus on Fiber Art: Selections from the Growing 20th-Century Collection*, The Art Institute of Chicago

1993-95 *Waves: Contemporary Japanese Fiberworks*, The Library and Gallery, Ontario, Canada

1995   *Contemporary Fiber Structure*, Joanne Rapp Gallery, Arizona, USA

          West/ Line/ East/ Space, Textile Arts Centre, Chicago

1995, 96 *2nd Textile Miniature Works '95, 18 x 18, Contemporary Art of Japan*, Gallery Gallery, Kyoto (tour Canada, Australia)

          Sheila Hicks Joined by Seven Friends and Colleagues from Japan, Brown/ Grotta Gallery, Connecticut, USA

1996   *Cinq Magiciens Textile du Japon*, Passage de Retz, Paris

1996, 97 *Textile Wizards from Japan*, The Israel Museum, Jerusalem

1997   *The 10th wave: A Celebration of the Brown/ Grotta Gallery's 10th Anniversary*, Brown/ Grotta Gallery, Connecticut, USA

1998   *Japanese Textile Miniature Exhibition, folding*, Canberra Museum and Gallery, Canberra (tour)

           Imaginations '98, Japanese Textile Miniature Exhibition, Gasthuiskapel, Poperinge, Belgium

1998-2001 *Structure and Surface: Contemporary Japanese Textiles*, The Museum of Modern Art, New York

           (tour USA, Canada, Garmany)

1999   *Seventy Designers in Tribute to Izzika Gaon*, The Israel Museum, Jerusalem

2000   *Kyoto City University of Arts, Exhibition in Commemoration of The 120th Anniversary of Its Founding*,

           Kyoto municipal Museum of Art, Kyoto

           Contemporary Japanese Textiles, Steendrukkerij Amsterdam, Amsterdam

2001   *Textural Space: Contemporary Japanese Textile Art*, James Hockey Gallery, Farnham, England (tour)

Selected Commissions and Design Works

1973   Mountain Villa of Fujita Industry Co., Ltd., Nasu

1978   Senri Chuoh Building, Taisho Fire & Marine Insurance Ltd., Osaka

1980   Keio Plaza Hotel, Tokyo

1980-81   Print works Stripes Series Prints, Art Kawashima Ltd., Tokyo

1993   Stage design for "Percussion Fantasia, Shitennoji Temple",

           Celebrating the 1400th Anniversary of Shitennoji Temple, Osaka

Work in Public Collections

           Museum of Arts and Crafts Hamburg, Hamburg

           The Art Institute of Chicago

           The Saint Louis Art Museum, Saint Louis, USA

           Stedelijk Museum, Amsterdam

           The Pulitzer Collection, Saint Louis, USA

           The Israel Museum, Jerusalem

           Passage de Retz, Paris

           Kyoto City University of Arts, Japan

Selected Publications and Reviews

1986   *On Chiyoko Tanaka's Works* (exhibition announcement), Ryo Gallery, Kyoto, essay by Shigeki Fukunaga

1987   *Expression/Construction of Filament* (exhibition catalogue), Spiral, Wacoal Art Center, Tokyo, essay by Shigeki Fukunaga

1989   *Art & Critique, Jan*, Kyoto, review by Rumi Yoshioka

       Decorative Design Journal, Jan, Tokyo, review by Shigeki Fukumoto

1991   *Senshoku Alpha, Mar*, Kyoto, "The World of Chiyoko Tanaka, Grinded Fabric", essay by Kiyoji Tsuji

1992   *Kohyama and Tanaka Contemporary Ceramics and Textile Art from Japan* (exhibition catalogue),
Museum het Princessehof, Leeuwarden, The Netherlands, essays by Shigeki Fukunaga and Marjan Unger

1996   *Atelier International, Oct*, Tokyo, review by Matthew Rose

       The Jerusalem Post Magazine, Nov, Jerusalem, review by Meir Ronnen

1997   *Surface Design Journal, Winter Issue*, California, "Surface in Japan: Beyond Traditional Technology",
essay by Glen Kaufman

       Art Textiles of the World: Japan, Telos Art Publishing, Winchester, England
essays by Keiko Kawashima and Matthew Koumis

1998   *Structure and Surface: Contemporary Japanese Textiles* (exhibition catalogue),
The Museum of Modern Art, New York, essays by Cara McCarty and Matilda McQuaid

       The New York Times, 20 Nov, New York, review by Grace Glueck

2001   *Textural Space: Contemporary Japanese Textile Art* (exhibition catalogue),
The Surrey Institute of Art & Design University College, Farnham, England

Professional

1997-   Kyoto City University of Arts, Kyoto

List of works

No.	Title	Year	Dimensions
1 (note 1)	Grinded Fabric – Ocher #300-1	1984-	507(w) x 100(d)cm
2 (note 1)	Grinded Fabric – Ocher #300-2	1984-	525(w) x 100(d)cm
3	Grinded Fabric – Six Squares, BG, Charcoal #402	1985	31.5 x 190cm
4	Mud Dyed Cloth – Permeated Black #400	1986	415(w) x 200(d)cm
5	Mud Dyed Cloth – Bengara #501	1984	28 x 36.5cm
6	Mud Dyed Cloth – Missing Mud Cross #764	1991	21.5 x 19cm
7	Printed and Grinded Fabric – Red Stripes On White Stripes #646	1985	28 x 29cm
8	Printed and Grinded Fabric – Red Stripes On White Stripes #647	1985	29 x 28cm
9	Printed and Grinded Fabric – Trace of White Line #641	1985	35 x 36cm
10	Printed and Grinded Fabric – White Line #642	1985	35 x 36cm
11	Printed and Grinded Fabric – Trace of A Leaf #151	1988	36 x 36cm
12 (note 2)	Grinded Fabric – Six Squares, Indigo Blue, W #306	1994	38.5 x 234cm
13 (note 2)	Grinded Fabric – Six Squares, Indigo Blue, RF #305	1994	38.5 x 234cm
14	Grinded Fabric – Blue #100-2	1983	98 x 134cm
15	Grinded Fabric – White, B #100-1	1983	428(w) x 98(d)cm
16	Grinded Fabric – Red Stripes, R #10	1988	202 x 100cm
17	Grinded Fabric – Three Squares, Blue Threads and Gray #671	1997	31.5 x 97.5cm
18	Grinded Fabric – Three Squares, Blue Threads and Sienna #281	1997	31.5 x 97cm
19 (note 3)	Permeated Black – Black Stain On Deep Green Stripes #53	1990	109.5 x 98cm
20	Permeated Black – Black Stains On Deep Green Stripes #52	1990	100 x 104.5cm
21	Permeated Black – Black Gradation #903	1990	234 x 37cm
22	Permeated Black – Six Squares, Black Gradation #904	1990	234.5 x 38.5cm
23	Kesa – *Sange*, Lotus Petals #97-1	1997	109.5 x 140.5cm
24	Kesa – *Sange*, Lotus Petals #97-3	1997	119 x 51cm
25	Kesa – *Sange*, Lotus Petals #97-4	1997	119 x 51cm
26	Kesa – *Sange*, Lotus Petals #98-1	1998	40.5 x 109cm

height x width (x depth)

(note 1)

This series has now been installed eight times, in various sites, over the past fourteen years. At each venue I have consistently used the same woven piece, '#300-2,' made with soil from my own prefecture. However, I have been compelled to use the resources available in the areas where the exhibitions were installed as substitution wefts for the original partner work, '#300-1.' In Kyoto I used soil from Jurakudai, an area in the south of Kyoto, for both sections but, for example, when the work was installed in Jerusalem I substituted sand collected from the surrounding deserts as the weft to complete the work.

Installation Venues and Dates:
1984 Gallery Gallery, Kyoto
1992 Museum het Princessehof, Leeuwarden, The Netherlands
       Museum für Kunst und Gewerbe Hamburg, Hamburg
1993 The Shiga Museum of Modern Art, Shiga
1995 AND Gallery, Kyoto
1996 Passage de Retz, Paris
1996, 97 The Israel Museum, Jerusalem
1998, 99 The Museum of Modern Art, New York

(note 2)

in the Public Collection of Kyoto City University of Arts

(note 3)

in the Public Collection of Passage de Retz, Paris

Other titles in this series

Vol 6: Anne Wilson
by Tim Porges and Hattie Gordon
This important American artist uses human hair, table linens and hand-stitching to probe poignant personal memories and histories, as well as evoking a subtle sense of landscape.
ISBN 1 902015 22 3 (softback)

Vol 7: Alice Kettle (February 2003)
by Dr Jennifer Harris
Get up close and intimate with recent major works by this Winchester-based painter who has become one of the world's most popular embroiderers.
ISBN 1 902015 31 2 (softback)
ISBN 1 902015 53 3 (hardback)

 Vol 8: Helen Lancaster (April 2002)
by Carolynne Skinner
The perilous fragility of nature, beautifully depicted by an outstanding conceptual environmentalist using paint, crochet, embroidery and fabric manipulation.
ISBN 1 902015 29 0 (softback)
ISBN 1 902015 45 2 (hardback)

Vol 9: Kay Lawrence (April 2002)
by Dr Diana Wood Conroy
One of the world's top tapestry weavers, her recent work negotiates issues about identity in textures ranging from minimal to lush, from sensuous to spiky.
ISBN 1 902015 28 2 (softback)
ISBN 1 902015 44 4 (hardback)

Vol 10: Joan Livingstone (April 2002)
by Gerry Craig
Livingstone's powerful installations incorporate felt, stitch and epoxy resin. Professor of Fiber and Material Studies in Chicago, she is one of America's most important sculptors.
ISBN 1 902015 27 4 (softback)
ISBN 1 902015 43 6 (hardback)

Vol 11: Marian Smit (April 2002)
by Marjolein v.d. Stoep
1st Prize winner in Third International Paper Triennal, Switzerland, 1999. "Work of great simplicity combining technique and poetry."
ISBN 1 902015 32 0 (softback)
ISBN 1 902015 46 0 (hardback)

Vol 12: Chiyoko Tanaka (April 2002)
by Lesley Millar
Tanaka's prized weavings are in public collections around the world. A leading light from Kyoto, her work is breathtaking and awe-inspiring.
ISBN 1 902015 24 X (softback)
ISBN 1 902015 42 8 (hardback)

Volume 14: Lia Cook (September 2002)
by Jenni Sorkin
Lia Cook's provocative weavings combine aspects of digital technology, painting and photography. Referencing diverse art histories, her images are distilled from a seemingly random movement of threads.
ISBN 1 902015 34 7 (softback)
ISBN 1 902015 51 7 (hardback)

Volume 15: Jane Lackey (September 2002)
by Irena Hofmann and Helga Pakasaar
Artist-in-residence at Cranbrook Academy of Art, her sculptural objects, installations and prints offer beguiling contemplations on the patterns, codes and maps of information concealed within the body.
ISBN 1 902015 35 5 (softback)
ISBN 1 902515 52 5 (hardback)

Please visit our website for details of all other volumes in this growing series.
www.arttextiles.com